Nora Roberts b[io]

A brief summary of the Life of a Legendary writer.

VEROJ PRESS

Copyright © 2023 Veroj press
All rights reserved. No part of this publication may be reproduced, distributed, or transmitted in any form or by any means, including photocopying, recording, or other electronic or mechanical methods, without the prior written permission of the publisher, except in the case of brief quotations embodied in critical reviews and certain other noncommercial uses permitted by copyright law.
This book is for educational and informational purposes only. It is not intended as a substitute for professional advice. The reader should always consult their professional advisors on any matter relating to their health, business, or personal life.

TABLE OF CONTENT

INTRODUCTION.

CHAPTER ONE: Early Life and Background.

CHAPTER TWO: Writing Career Beginnings.

CHAPTER THREE: Breakthrough Novel and Success.

CHAPTER FOUR: Personal Life and Relationships.

CHAPTER FIVE: Writing Style and Themes.

CHAPTER SIX: Literary Awards and Recognition.

CHAPTER SEVEN: Philanthropy and Charity Work.

CHAPTER EIGHT: Controversies and Criticisms.

CHAPTER NINE: Legacy and Impact.

CONCLUSION.

INTRODUCTION

Nora Roberts, born Eleanor Marie Robertson, is a renowned American author who has captivated readers around the world with her gripping and emotional storytelling. With over 200 novels to her name and 750 million copies in print, Roberts has become one of the best-selling authors of all time. Her works span various genres, including romance, mystery, suspense, and fantasy, and she is known for her strong and relatable characters, intricate plotlines, and richly detailed settings.

Born on October 10, 1950, in Silver Spring, Maryland, Roberts grew up in a blue-collar family. From a young age, she showed a keen interest in literature and storytelling, often immersing herself in books and weaving her own tales. It was her mother, a book lover herself, who nurtured Roberts's love for reading and encouraged her to pursue her passion for writing.

After graduating from high school, Roberts attended Montgomery College, where she studied journalism. However, she soon discovered that her true calling lay in crafting stories rather than reporting them. This realization led her to change her course and pursue a career as a novelist. Little did she know that this decision would pave the way for an extraordinary literary journey.

In the early years of her writing career, Roberts faced numerous rejections from publishers, but she refused to give up. Undeterred by setbacks, she continued honing her writing skills and refining

her unique voice. Her perseverance paid off when, in 1981, her debut novel, "Irish Thoroughbred," was published under her pen name, Nora Roberts. The book was an instant success and marked the beginning of her remarkable rise to literary stardom.

Roberts's storytelling prowess and ability to create vibrant and relatable characters quickly garnered a dedicated fan base. Her novels often explore themes of love, family, self-discovery, and personal growth, resonating with readers on a deep emotional level. Whether it is through her heartwarming romance novels or her intense suspense and mystery stories, Roberts has an uncanny ability to transport readers into her fictional worlds, making them feel as if they are part of the journey themselves.

Beyond her captivating storytelling, Roberts is also known for her prolific output. She writes under several pen names, including J.D. Robb for her popular "In Death" series, which combines elements of romance, suspense, and futuristic crime. With such versatility, she continuously keeps her readers engaged and eager for more.

Despite her immense success and popularity, Roberts remains a humble and down-to-earth individual. She values her privacy and maintains a close-knit family life. Married to Bruce Wilder, a carpenter, she has two sons, both of whom have inherited her love for writing and storytelling.

In addition to her literary achievements, Roberts is also actively involved in philanthropy and charity work. She has established the

Nora Roberts Foundation, which supports various causes such as literacy, hunger, and cancer research. Her generosity extends to supporting aspiring writers through scholarships and mentorship programs.

With her enduring legacy and incredible contribution to the literary world, Nora Roberts has solidified her place as a true icon. Her ability to captivate readers with her poignant and inspiring tales has earned her a special place in the hearts of millions. From her humble beginnings to her extraordinary success, Roberts's journey is a testament to the power of perseverance, passion, and the incredible impact of storytelling.

CHAPTER ONE: Early Life and Background

Nora Roberts, born Eleanor Marie Robertson, was born on October 10, 1950, in Silver Spring, Maryland. She grew up in a blue-collar family, with her father working as a plumber and her mother as a homemaker. From a young age, Roberts showed a natural talent for storytelling and a deep love for books.

Raised in a household that valued education, Roberts's mother encouraged her to read voraciously and explore various literary genres. This early exposure to literature sparked her imagination and ignited her passion for storytelling. Roberts would spend countless hours immersed in books, captivated by the worlds and characters created by other authors.

Following her graduation from high school, Roberts enrolled in Montgomery College, where she studied journalism. However, she soon realized that her true calling was not in reporting the news, but in crafting stories of her own. Inspired by the works of authors such as Jane Austen and Daphne du Maurier, she decided to pursue a career as a novelist.

Like many aspiring writers, Roberts faced her fair share of challenges and rejections in the early years of her writing career. Publishers were hesitant to take a chance on a new author, but Roberts refused to be discouraged. She diligently honed her craft, refining her writing skills and developing her unique voice.

In 1981, Roberts's persistence paid off when her debut novel, "Irish Thoroughbred," was published. This marked the beginning of her remarkable literary journey and the birth of her pen name, Nora Roberts. The book was well-received by readers and set the stage for her subsequent success.

Roberts's early life experiences and personal beliefs often shape the themes she explores in her novels. Growing up in a close-knit family, she places great importance on the value of love, relationships, and personal growth. These aspects are pronounced in many of her stories, where she delves into the complexities of family dynamics, the transformative power of love, and the resilience of the human spirit.

While she is primarily known for her romance novels, Roberts's versatility as a writer is evident in her ability to seamlessly transition between different genres. From mystery and suspense to fantasy and science fiction, Roberts has demonstrated her range and ability to captivate readers across various literary landscapes.

Today, Nora Roberts is one of the most successful authors in the world, with a devoted fan base that spans continents. Her impressive body of work, which includes over 200 novels and countless short stories, has sold millions of copies and continues to enchant readers with its richly detailed characters and compelling narratives.

Despite her immense success, Roberts remains grounded and appreciative of her achievements. She values her privacy and maintains a balanced family life with her husband and two children. Alongside her writing career, Roberts is also actively involved in philanthropy, using her success to make a positive impact in the lives of others through her foundation and support of various charitable causes.

From her humble beginnings in Maryland to becoming a literary icon, Nora Roberts's early life and background have played a significant role in shaping her as both a person and a writer. Her passion, dedication, and unwavering commitment to her craft have cemented her status as one of the most beloved and influential authors of our time.

CHAPTER TWO: Writing Career Beginnings:

Nora Roberts's writing career began with a passion for storytelling and a determination to share her stories with the world. From an early age, she immersed herself in books, finding solace and inspiration within the pages of novels. It was this love for literature that eventually led her to pursue a career as a writer. As a young woman, Roberts studied journalism at Montgomery College, intending to pursue a career in reporting. However, she quickly realized that her true passion lay in creating her own stories, rather than reporting the news. It was during this time that she made the pivotal decision to redirect her focus toward fiction writing.

In the early years of her writing career, Roberts faced numerous challenges and rejections. Publishers were hesitant to take a chance on a new and unknown author. However, Roberts refused to be discouraged. She diligently worked on her craft, continuously honing her writing skills and refining her storytelling abilities.

Despite the initial setbacks, Roberts's persistence eventually paid off when her debut novel, "Irish Thoroughbred," was published in 1981. This marked the beginning of an incredibly prolific writing career that would span several decades and establish her as a bestselling author.

From that point forward, Roberts's career took off, with her novels garnering immense popularity and capturing the hearts of readers worldwide. She demonstrated remarkable versatility as a writer, exploring various genres such as romance, mystery, suspense, fantasy, and science fiction. This versatility allowed her to continuously captivate readers and maintain a loyal following.

Roberts's writing style is characterized by vivid storytelling, well-developed characters, and richly imagined worlds. Her ability to create relatable and engaging characters has been key to her success, as readers often find themselves emotionally invested in the lives and journeys of her protagonists.

Throughout her writing career, Roberts has remained committed to honing her craft and pushing the boundaries of her storytelling. Her dedication to her readers and her desire to provide them with immersive and fulfilling reading experiences is evident in the wealth of novels she has produced.

With over 200 novels and countless short stories to her name, Nora Roberts has firmly established herself as one of the most successful and influential writers of our time. Her novels have sold millions of copies worldwide and have been translated into numerous languages. She has received numerous accolades and awards for her contributions to the literary world.

Roberts's writing career beginnings set the stage for her immense success. Her passion for storytelling, combined with her tenacity
and resilience, propelled her forward through the challenges she faced. Today, she continues to inspire aspiring writers, showing them that with dedication, perseverance, and a belief in their own voices, they too can make their dreams of becoming successful authors a reality.

CHAPTER THREE: Breakthrough Novel and Success

Nora Roberts experienced a breakthrough in her writing career with the publication of her novel "Morrigan's Cross" in 2006. This novel marked a significant turning point for Roberts, propelling her into even greater success and solidifying her position as a bestselling author.

"Morrigan's Cross" is the first book in the Circle Trilogy, a captivating blend of romance, fantasy, and paranormal elements. The novel introduces readers to a magical world where sorcery, vampires, and mythical beings converge. It tells the story of Hoyt Mac Cionaoith, a man who is chosen to be part of a group known as the Circle, destined to battle an ancient evil force threatening to destroy humanity.

The novel's release was met with immense enthusiasm from readers, who were captivated by its mesmerizing blend of genres, engaging characters, and thrilling plotlines. "Morrigan's Cross" quickly climbed the bestseller lists and received rave reviews,

cementing Roberts's status as a master storyteller who could seamlessly weave different genres together.

The success of "Morrigan's Cross" sparked a trend of fantasy-infused romance novels in Roberts's career, with subsequent series such as the Key Trilogy and the Guardians Trilogy further exploring magical realms and mythical adventures. Roberts's ability to captivate readers with her unique blend of romance and fantasy set her apart as a distinct and influential voice in the literary world.

Furthermore, the success of "Morrigan's Cross" opened doors for Roberts to explore new avenues in her writing career. She began penning futuristic suspense novels under the pseudonym J.D. Robb, introducing readers to the gritty and captivating world of Lieutenant Eve Dallas in the "In Death" series. This foray into the crime fiction genre proved to be another breakthrough for Roberts, further expanding her readership and solidifying her status as a versatile and accomplished author.

The breakthrough success of "Morrigan's Cross" also allowed Roberts to expand her literary empire. She collaborated with other authors on several novel trilogies, which further showcased her storytelling abilities and provided readers with exciting and fresh narratives.

The success of "Morrigan's Cross" and its subsequent sequels not only propelled Roberts's career to new heights but also opened

doors for other authors writing in the romance and fantasy genres. Her ability to bring diverse genres together and create richly imagined worlds has left an indelible mark on the literary landscape.

CHAPTER FOUR: Personal Life and Relationships:

Nora Roberts, in addition to her notable achievements in the literary world, also has a fulfilling personal life and successful relationships. Despite her busy schedule and demanding career, she has managed to cultivate a strong support system and maintain meaningful connections with her loved ones.

Roberts has been married to her husband, Bruce Wilder, since 1985. Their marriage has been a cornerstone of her personal life, providing her with a loving and stable partnership. Together, they have raised two children, both of whom have grown up to lead successful lives of their own. The longevity and strength of Roberts's marriage reflect her commitment to building and nurturing strong relationships.

Family is of utmost importance to Roberts, and she values the close bonds she shares with her loved ones. She often credits her upbringing and the support of her family for her success and ability to pursue her passions. Roberts's dedication to her family is evident in the way she incorporates the theme of familial love and loyalty into her novels, adding an authentic touch to her storytelling.

In addition to her immediate family, Roberts has developed deep friendships throughout her life, which have become an essential part of her support system. These friendships provide her with a network of trust, understanding, and companionship, allowing her to navigate the ups and downs of life with greater resilience. Roberts's ability to maintain lasting friendships demonstrates her genuine care for others and her commitment to nurturing meaningful connections.

Despite her fame and success, Roberts remains down-to-earth and approachable. She engages with her readers through social media platforms and attends book signings and events, connecting directly with her fans. Roberts's genuine interest in her readers and her willingness to engage with them on a personal level has endeared her to a vast and loyal fan base.

Furthermore, Roberts understands the importance of giving back to the community and uses her influence to make a positive impact. She is an active philanthropist, supporting various charitable organizations and causes. Roberts's charitable efforts range from addressing literacy issues to supporting organizations that empower women and children. Through her philanthropic endeavors, she not only improves the lives of others but also inspires her readers to get involved and make a difference.

In summary, Nora Roberts's personal life and relationships are as integral to her success as her writing. Her strong and enduring marriage, close-knit family, and meaningful friendships provide her with a support system that fuels her creativity and resilience.

Additionally, Roberts's genuine connection with her readers and dedication to giving back to the community further exemplify her commitment to fostering meaningful relationships and making a positive impact. Nora Roberts's personal life and relationships are a testament to her authenticity, kindness, and unwavering dedication to both her craft and the people who have shaped her life.

CHAPTER FIVE: Writing Style and Themes:

Nora Roberts is celebrated not only for her engaging storytelling but also for her unique writing style and the compelling themes she explores in her novels. Her distinct style and the themes she delves

into have contributed to her immense popularity and the timeless appeal of her works.

Roberts's writing style is characterized by its fluidity, descriptive flair, and ability to transport readers into vividly imagined worlds. Her prose is polished and accessible, allowing readers to effortlessly immerse themselves in the stories she weaves. Whether it's a romantic scene that melts hearts or a suspenseful moment that keeps readers on the edge of their seats, Roberts has an innate ability to captivate and hold her audience's attention.

One of the central themes that runs through many of Roberts's novels is the power of love and the resilience of the human spirit. She expertly explores the complexities of interpersonal relationships, delving into the depths of human emotions and experiences. From the euphoria of falling in love to the challenges and sacrifices that come with enduring relationships, Roberts paints a realistic and heartfelt portrayal of love in all its forms.

Another recurring theme in Roberts's works is the importance of family. She highlights the dynamics between family members and the bonds that tie them together. Roberts delves into the dynamics of sibling relationships, exploring the complexities of sibling rivalries and the unbreakable support systems that siblings provide each other. She also explores the transformative power of parenthood, touching on the joys and challenges of raising children and the sacrifices parents make for their families.

Roberts also incorporates elements of suspense, mystery, and danger into her novels, crossing genres and keeping readers enthralled with intricate plotlines. She often includes elements of crime, thriller, or the supernatural, adding another layer of intrigue to her stories. Roberts's ability to seamlessly blend romance, suspense, and mystery has made her novels highly addictive and appealing to a wide range of readers.

Additionally, multiculturalism and diversity are recurring themes in Roberts's works. She embraces and celebrates characters from different ethnicities and backgrounds, allowing readers to experience different cultures and perspectives. Roberts showcases the richness and diversity of the world we live in, promoting understanding and appreciation for different cultures and traditions.

Furthermore, Roberts has a talent for creating compelling female protagonists who are strong, independent, and multifaceted. Her heroines are not simply damsels in distress but powerful women who overcome adversity, pursue their dreams, and stand up for what they believe in. By portraying strong female characters, Roberts empowers her readers and encourages women to embrace their own strength and agency.

In summary, Nora Roberts's writing style is characterized by its captivating and effortless storytelling. Her themes touch upon the power of love, the importance of family, the allure of suspense and mystery, and the celebration of multiculturalism and diversity. Through her masterful storytelling and exploration of these themes, Roberts has become a beloved author whose novels continue to resonate with readers around the world.

CHAPTER SIX: Literary Awards and Recognition:

Nora Roberts, one of the most prolific and beloved authors of our time, has received numerous literary awards and recognition throughout her career. Her extraordinary contributions to the romance genre and her exceptional storytelling skills have earned her a well-deserved place in the literary world.

One of the most prestigious awards that Nora Roberts has received is the Romance Writers of America (RWA) Lifetime Achievement Award. This honor, bestowed upon her in 1997, acknowledges her remarkable achievements and lasting impact on the romance genre. As a pioneer in the field, Roberts has captivated readers with her intricate plots, well-developed characters, and engrossing love stories. The RWA Lifetime Achievement Award recognizes her immense influence on the genre and her dedication to crafting evocative tales of love and romance.

In addition to the RWA Lifetime Achievement Award, Nora Roberts has also been recognized by the Romance Writers of America with the RITA Award, the highest honor in the genre. She has received this prestigious award on several occasions, underscoring her consistent excellence in crafting compelling stories that resonate with readers. The RITA Award showcases Roberts' mastery of the romance genre and her ability to create captivating narratives that touch the hearts of millions.

Furthermore, Nora Roberts has received recognition beyond the realm of romance literature. In 2007, she was inducted into the Romance Writers of America Hall of Fame, a testament to her enduring contribution to the genre. This accolade acknowledges her status as a trailblazer and visionary, whose work has redefined and elevated the romance genre.

Nora Roberts' literary achievements have not gone unnoticed by the broader literary community. She has been honored with the Quill Award, which recognizes outstanding works in various genres. In 2005, she received the Quills Book of the Year Award for her novel "Angels Fall," further solidifying her position as a gifted and beloved author across genres.

Beyond awards, Nora Roberts' books have consistently topped

bestseller lists, with countless works reaching the coveted number one spot. Her remarkable commercial success and dedicated fan base are testaments to the impact her writing has had on readers worldwide. Roberts' ability to consistently deliver engaging stories that blend romance, suspense, and gripping plots has made her a household name and a true literary icon.

In summary, Nora Roberts' literary awards and recognition highlight her exceptional talent and dedication to storytelling. From prestigious honors like the RWA

Lifetime Achievement Award and the RITA Award to induction into the Romance Writers of America Hall of Fame, Roberts' impact on the romance genre cannot be overstated. Her ability to create captivating narratives and touch the hearts of readers has earned her a place among the most celebrated authors of our time.

CHAPTER SEVEN: Philanthropy and Charity Work:

Beyond her remarkable literary accomplishments, Nora

Roberts is also known for her philanthropy and charity work, demonstrating her commitment to making a positive impact on the world.

One of the significant charitable endeavors that Nora Roberts has been involved in is her support for literacy initiatives. Recognizing the power of reading and education, she has donated millions of dollars to various organizations that promote literacy and provide access to books for underprivileged children and adults. Roberts understands that literacy is the key to empowerment and has actively contributed to initiatives that ensure that everyone has the opportunity to experience the joy and benefits of reading.

Furthermore, Roberts is a strong advocate for the arts and has made substantial contributions to organizations and programs that support artistic development. She understands the transformative power of creativity and believes in fostering and nurturing artistic talent, especially among young people. Roberts has provided generous donations to support scholarships, workshops, and educational programs that encourage artistic expression and enable individuals to pursue their creative passions.

Additionally, Roberts has shown a keen commitment to animal welfare. She has extended her philanthropy to organizations that rescue, rehabilitate, and provide care for animals in need. By supporting animal shelters and sanctuaries, Roberts has made a significant impact in improving the lives of countless animals, ensuring they receive the care, love, and attention they deserve.

Moreover, Roberts has been actively involved in supporting local communities and organizations. Whether it is providing financial aid, volunteering her time, or lending her voice to various causes, she consistently demonstrates her dedication to creating positive change. From supporting food banks and homeless shelters to contributing to disaster relief efforts, Roberts has shown that she understands the importance of giving back and making a difference in the lives of others.

In recognition of her philanthropic spirit and commitment to making the world a better place, Nora Roberts has been honored with several awards and accolades. She has been recognized for her philanthropic contributions by organizations such as the Library of Congress, the Association of American Publishers, and other notable institutions.

Overall, Nora Roberts' philanthropy and charity work exemplify her compassionate nature and her belief in the power of making a difference. Through her generosity and dedication, she has had a positive impact on numerous lives, resonating far beyond the pages of her novels. Nora Roberts serves as an inspiration, not only as a gifted writer but also as a compassionate and socially conscious individual, using her success to transform lives and communities for the better.

CHAPTER EIGHT: Controversies and Criticisms:

While Nora Roberts enjoys immense popularity and success as a renowned author, she has not been immune to controversies and criticisms throughout her career.

One area of criticism that Roberts has faced relates to the repetitive nature of her storytelling. Some argue that her novels follow a similar formula, often featuring strong female protagonists, romantic storylines, and suspenseful plotlines. Critics claim that this formulaic approach can make her books predictable and lacking in originality. However, Roberts' fans appreciate her consistent storytelling style and often view it as a comforting aspect of her work.

Another controversy that has surrounded Nora Roberts is the accusation of plagiarism. Over the years, there have been several instances where Roberts has been accused of borrowing elements from other authors' works without proper attribution. In one notable case, Roberts was accused of plagiarizing from fellow romance author Janet Dailey. Although Roberts maintained that any similarities were coincidental, the controversy sparked a public dispute between the two authors. While plagiarism accusations remain rare in Roberts' extensive body of work, these incidents have caused some to question the originality and integrity of her writing.

Furthermore, some critics argue that Roberts' books perpetuate unrealistic or outdated gender dynamics. They contend that her male characters often possess traditional, stereotypical traits, while her female characters are portrayed as strong and capable yet still dependent on male love interests. This imbalance, critics argue, reinforces gender roles and fails to challenge societal norms and expectations. However, it is important to note that Roberts has also written books with complex and empowered female characters who defy stereotypes, showcasing a range of portrayals.

Lastly, Roberts has faced criticism for the lack of diversity in her novels. Many argue that her stories predominantly feature white, heterosexual characters, neglecting to include marginalized backgrounds or LGBTQ+

representation. While some argue that
Roberts' focus on romantic relationships may limit her ability to explore a wider range of characters, it is important for authors to strive for inclusivity and accurately reflect the diverse world we live in.

Despite these controversies and criticisms, Nora Roberts continues to captivate readers worldwide with her engaging storytelling and immense storytelling talent. While her work may not be without its flaws, she remains a beloved author to countless fans who appreciate the emotional depth and escape her novels provide. As with any successful artist, it is inevitable that Roberts will encounter criticism, and it is up to individual readers to decide whether they resonate with her stories and writing style.

CHAPTER NINE: Legacy and Impact:

Nora Roberts has undeniably left a lasting legacy on the literary world and has had a significant impact on both the romance genre and the publishing industry as a whole.

One of the most notable aspects of Roberts' legacy is her incredible productivity. With over 200 novels to her name, she has consistently been able to provide her fans with engaging stories while maintaining a high level of quality. Through her dedication and work ethic, Roberts has set a standard for prolific writing that has inspired and influenced countless authors.

In addition to her prolific output, Roberts has also played a crucial role in shaping the romance genre. Her novels have not only entertained readers but have also brought broader recognition to the genre. Roberts has shown that romance novels can be just as complex, well-written, and emotionally resonant as any other literary work, debunking the stigma often associated with the genre.

Furthermore, Roberts' success has had a significant impact on the publishing world. Her novels consistently top bestseller lists, demonstrating her ability to connect with readers on a wide scale. This success has influenced publishers to invest more in romance authors and has paved the way for other romance writers to gain widespread recognition and success. Roberts' achievements have also opened doors for women in the industry, highlighting the power of female authors in shaping the literary landscape.

Beyond her literary accomplishments, Roberts has also made a significant impact through her philanthropy. As a supporter of literacy and education, she has established the Nora Roberts

Foundation, which focuses on programs that support literacy, arts, and children's programs. Roberts has used her success and influence to give back to the community and make a positive difference in the lives of others.

Moreover, Roberts' books have provided readers with an escape from reality and offered comfort during difficult times. Her ability to create intricate worlds and compelling characters has allowed readers to lose themselves in her stories, finding solace and inspiration within the pages of her novels.

Overall, Nora Roberts' legacy and impact are profound. Her writing has entertained and captivated millions of readers worldwide, challenging preconceptions about the romance genre along the way. Through her success, she has influenced the publishing industry and paved the way for other romance authors. Additionally, Roberts' commitment to philanthropy has showcased her generosity and dedication to making the world a better place. Nora Roberts will be remembered as not only a master storyteller but also a trailblazing author who has left an indelible mark on the literary world.

CONCLUSION

Nora Roberts has established herself as a literary powerhouse and an icon in the publishing industry. Her legacy will forever be marked by her unwavering dedication to her craft, her ability to consistently produce high-quality work, and her influence in shaping the romance genre.

Roberts' impact on the literary world cannot be overstated. With her extensive bibliography of over 200 novels, she has brought joy and entertainment to millions of readers worldwide. Her stories have transcended genre boundaries, captivating readers with their complex characters, intricate plots, and heartfelt emotions.

Through her writing, Roberts has shown that romance novels can be powerful works of literature that resonate with readers on a profound level.

Not only has Roberts revolutionized the romance genre, but she has also made a lasting impact on the publishing industry as a whole. Her unprecedented success has shattered stereotypes and proven that women authors, particularly in the romance genre, can achieve great heights. Her ability to consistently top bestseller lists and capture the hearts of readers has opened doors for countless authors, allowing them to gain recognition and success in a highly competitive industry.

Beyond her literary achievements, Roberts' philanthropic work exemplifies her generous spirit and commitment to making a

difference. Through the Nora Roberts Foundation, she has supported programs that promote literacy, the arts, and children's education. Her dedication to giving back to the community is a testament to her character and the positive influence she seeks to have both on and off the page.

Roberts' enduring legacy is not only in the number of books she has written or the accolades she has received but in the impact she has had on the lives of her readers. Her novels have provided an escape from reality, offering comfort, inspiration, and a renewed sense of hope. Through her stories, Roberts has touched the hearts of

readers, fostering a sense of connection and reminding us of the power of love and resilience.

As her fans eagerly anticipate each new release, it is clear that Nora

Roberts' influence and legacy will continue to thrive for generations to come. Her talent, dedication, and passion for storytelling have left an indelible mark on the literary world, inspiring both readers and fellow authors to pursue their own creative endeavors. Nora Roberts will forever be remembered as a trailblazer and a master storyteller, whose words have the power to transport us to new worlds, ignite our imaginations, and remind us of the enduring power of love.

THE END.

Printed in Great Britain
by Amazon